People Around the World

Life and Culture in

EAST AND SOUTHEAST

ASIA

HOLLY BROWN

PowerKiDS press.

Published in 2021 by The Rosen Publishing Group, Inc.
29 East 21st Street, New York, NY 10010

First Edition

Editor: Siyavush Saidian
Book Design: Seth Hughes

Photo Credits: Cover wong yu liang/Shutterstock.com; p. 5 Rudy Balasko/Shutterstock.com; p. 7 (left) © Istockphoto/phanthit; p. 7 (right) fotosen55/Shutterstock.com; p. 8 (left) Sakdawut Tangtongsap/Shutterstock.com; p. 8 (right) © Istockphoto/sihasakprachum; p. 10 Babbage/ Wikimedia Commons; p. 11 © Istockphoto/Pramote2015; p. 13 (left) © Istockphoto/ gagarych; p. 13 (right) Sony Herdiana/Shutterstock.com; p. 15 AngelaGrant/Shutterstock.com; p. 16 © Istockphoto/bee32; p. 17 © Istockphoto/loeskieboom; p. 19 (top) H. O. Havemeyer Collection, Bequest of Mrs. H. O. Havemeyer, 1929/The Metropolitan Museum of Art; p. 19 (bottom) © Istockphoto/woraput; p. 20 Atiwat Witthayanurut/Shutterstock.com; p. 21 (left) © Istockphoto/Neil Bussey; p. 21 (right) MooNam StockPhoto/Shutterstock.com; p. 22 JStone/ Shutterstock.com; p. 25 (top) YOSHIKAZU TSUNO/Contributor/Gamma-Rapho/Getty Images; p. 25 (bottom) surassawadee/Shutterstock.com; p. 27 Bettmann/Contributor/Bettmann/ Getty Images; p. 28 © Istockphoto/ake1150sb; p. 30 © Istockphoto/narvikk; p. 32–35 Max Roser, Hannah Ritchie and Esteban Ortiz-Ospina (2020) - "World Population Growth". *Published online at OurWorldInData.org.* Retrieved from: 'https://ourworldindata.org/world-population-growth' [Online Resource]; p. 36 (left) Nikontiger/E+/Getty Images; p. 36 (right) © Istockphoto/SeanPavonePhoto; p. 37 think4photop/Shutterstock.com; p. 38 © Istockphoto/ RyuSeungil; p. 39 © Istockphoto/malo85; p. 41 © Istockphoto/Chaiyaporn1144; p. 42 Suzanne Pratt/Shutterstock.com; p. 43 Korkusung/Shutterstock.com; p. 44 TonyV3112/ Shutterstock.com; p. 45 David Kucera/Shutterstock.com.

Cataloging-in-Publication Data
Names: Brown, Holly.
Title: Life and culture in East and Southeast Asia / Holly Brown.
Description: New York : PowerKids Press, 2021. | Series: People around the world | Includes glossary and index.
Identifiers: ISBN 9781725321809 (pbk.) | ISBN 9781725321823 (library bound) | ISBN 9781725321816 (6 pack) | ISBN 9781725321830 (ebook)
Subjects: LCSH: East Asia–Juvenile literature. | Southeast Asia–Juvenile literature. | East Asia– Social life and customs–Juvenile literature. | East Asia–Civilization–Juvenile literature. | Southeast Asia–Social life and customs–Juvenile literature.
Classification: LCC DS509.3 B769 2021 | DDC 951–dc23

Manufactured in the United States of America

CPSIA Compliance Information: Batch #CSPK20: For Further Information contact Rosen Publishing, New York, New York at 1-800-237-9932

Find us on

Contents

Introduction
WHAT IS CULTURE?

The region of east and Southeast Asia is rich with culture, or ways of life of a group of people. Culture is seen in the festive celebrations of Chinese New Year and the unique seafood cuisine of Japan. Cultural features are influenced by the region's geography, including the Himalayas, the Gobi Desert of China and Mongolia, and the island nations of Indonesia and the Philippines. For thousands of years, geographical challenges kept many cultures isolated, so they developed unique religions, art, and languages. Trade and travel, from the Silk Road to today, led to **cultural diffusion**.

East Asia includes the countries of the People's Republic of China (often called China), the Republic of China (often called Taiwan), Japan, North Korea, South Korea, and Mongolia.

cultural diffusion: The process of spreading cultural traits from one region to another.

The Tokyo skyline shows both the traditional temples and modern architecture that contribute to Japan's distinctive culture.

Macau and Hong Kong are sometimes considered independent countries, though they are technically part of China. Southeast Asia includes Cambodia, Vietnam, Laos, Thailand, Myanmar (formerly Burma), Malaysia, Indonesia, Brunei, Timor-Leste, the Philippines, and the **city-state** of Singapore.

Throughout history, people from each nation have moved and mixed with their neighbors, transforming local cultures. Each country also maintains its own long-standing traditions while continuing to change with the influence of **globalization**.

1

PAST AND PRESENT CULTURAL CONTRIBUTIONS

Some of the oldest events in human history happened in east and Southeast Asia. The first east Asian civilization existed in China around 11,000 years ago. The ancient Chinese developed important philosophical ideas, such as **Confucianism**, that are still studied in Asia today. They also invented some of the most important tools in history, such as the compass, gunpowder, and clocks.

Strongly influenced by ancient China, ancient Japanese civilization is also credited with many important cultural contributions. *Noh*, a traditional Japanese style of theater, has been performed since the 1400s, making it the oldest surviving theatrical style in the world.

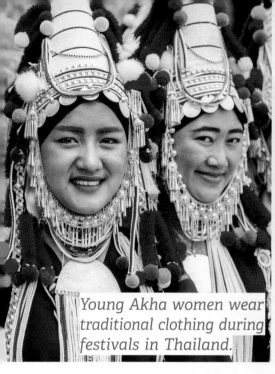

Young Akha women wear traditional clothing during festivals in Thailand.

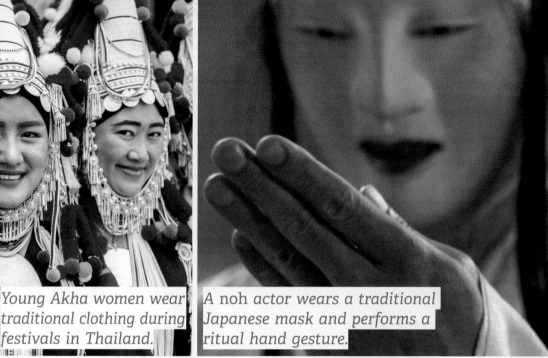

A noh actor wears a traditional Japanese mask and performs a ritual hand gesture.

Today, most Southeast Asians are descended from east and central Asians who migrated during ancient times, bringing their ideals and traditions with them. **Indigenous** people, such as the Akha, the Hmong, and many other hill tribes, still live in remote areas of northern Thailand, Laos, Myanmar, and Vietnam.

CULTURAL CONNECTIONS

In the early 1600s, Japan decided to stop outside influence and close its borders to the world. In 1853, as a show of force, U.S. naval officer Matthew Perry sailed a warship to Tokyo. Japan agreed to open two ports of trade to the United States in 1854.

*Many Buddhist monks still make **pilgrimages** to ancient temples, such as Angkor Wat in Cambodia.*

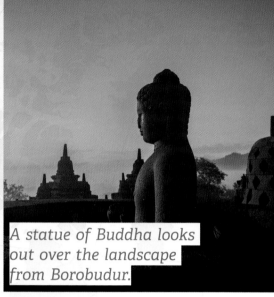

A statue of Buddha looks out over the landscape from Borobudur.

Some of the world's most impressive ancient monuments are found in Southeast Asia. Angkor Wat, located in Cambodia, was built by the ancient Khmer people in the 1100s. It is the world's largest religious structure. Borobudur—a massive Buddhist temple in central Java, Indonesia—and the ancient, abandoned city of Bagan in Myanmar are two more archaeological treasures and important historical sites in Southeast Asia. These incredible structures serve as monuments to Asia's ancient cultures.

While ancient traditions influence much of east and Southeast Asia today, it's impossible to ignore the effects of **imperialism** on the culture of Southeast Asia. The Silk Road trading

imperialism: A policy by which a country increases its power by gaining control over other areas of the world.

Thailand was the only country in Southeast Asia to remain free during the age of imperialism. The British took control of parts of Brunei, Singapore, Malaysia, and Myanmar; the French controlled Vietnam, Cambodia, and Laos; the Dutch controlled Indonesia; the Portuguese controlled what is now Timor-Leste; and the Spanish controlled the Philippines.

routes between Europe and China were established around the 2nd century BC. The Silk Road was the most popular trade route until the 15th century AD, but the routes continued being used through the 17th century. The 16th century marked the

Multiculturalism in Indonesia

Indonesia is made up of more than 17,500 islands, which cover more than 3,200 miles (5,149.9 km). The country has the fourth-largest population in the world. The people of Indonesia belong to 300 different ethnic groups. Indonesians speak hundreds of languages, including the official language, Bahasa Indonesia, which serves as a common language shared between different groups. Indonesia is a multicultural society. The nation shows great pride in the many traditions that have shaped Indonesian culture. Its national motto is *Bhinneka Tunggal Ika*, which translates to "Unity in Diversity."

beginning of European entrepôts, or trading posts, in Southeast Asia. By the 18th century, Europeans began taking control of the region.

The Silk Road

The Silk Road was a collection of trade routes that stretched more than 4,000 miles (6,437.4 km), connecting China to the Mediterranean Sea. It was called the Silk Road because of the huge amounts of silk it helped transport from China to Europe. China also sent porcelain, tea, and medicine to Europe and received goods like wool, linen, and wine in return. Because the Silk Road allowed people to travel through areas with many different cultures, it helped exchange not only goods but also new ideas and cultural practices. Different religions, the study of algebra and astronomy, printmaking, medical techniques, and even the Arabic number system all spread through the Silk Road.

This map shows how far the Silk Road stretched through Asia and beyond. It connected two major empires—the Chinese and the Roman.

Massalia
Rome
Italy
Panticapaeum
Constantinople
Scythia
Black Sea
Sogdia
Yining
Turpan
Anxi County
Luoyang
Ningbo
Antioch
Caspian Sea
Samarkand
Kokand
Aksu
Dunhuang
Wuwei
Chang'an
Hangzhou
Tyre
Dura-Europos
Aria
Kashgar
Hotan
Fuzhou
Libya
Merv
Bactria
China
Alexandria
Damascus
Qumis, Iran
Balch
Bagram
Quanzhou
Селевкия
-Ктесифон
Persia
Taxila
Charsadda
Guangzhou
Africa
Egypt
Persian Gulf
Gedrosia
Махтура
Pataliputra
Arabia
Tamluk
India
Aden
Амаратави
Ок-Ео
Machilipatnam
Ethiopia

Silk Road
Circa 1st century CE

— Main route of Silk Road
— Other caravan route

Many Southeast Asians disliked imperialism, and after World War II ended in 1945, many nations began to fight for—and win—their independence.

This monument in Laos shows the European influence on traditional styles of east Asian architecture.

Ancient traditions, large-scale migration, and the long-lasting effects of imperialism have heavily influenced the cultures of east and Southeast Asia. The languages of colonial nations are still widely spoken throughout the region, and Christianity and Islam are widespread. The rich histories of the regions' politics, religions, foods, and natural environments still live on today.

2 PHILOSOPHICAL IDEAS AND RELIGIONS

Buddhism is the most practiced religion in east and Southeast Asia, and it has between 350 million and 500 million followers worldwide. Believers follow the teachings of the Buddha, a legendary prince who found **enlightenment** after giving up his wealth. He spent the rest of his life teaching his philosophies. These teachings are called dharma, and they tell followers that

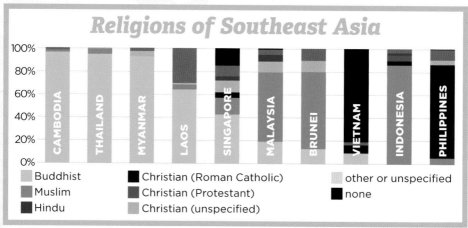

While Buddhism and Islam are popular across Southeast Asia, this graph shows that other religions are widely recognized as well.

enlightenment: A state of spiritual perfection.

every person is born again after they die and that the quality of future lives is based on the good or bad things done in past lives. Followers try to break this cycle of rebirth by giving up desires and wealth to reach **nirvana**. Buddhism is widely practiced in Japan, China, South Korea, Taiwan, Thailand, Laos, Cambodia, Myanmar, and Vietnam, but it looks a little different in every country.

Shown here are Buddhist monks meditating in front of Buddha at Phan Tao Temple in Chiang Mai, Thailand.

Muslims gather to pray outside of Garut Grand Mosque in Java, Indonesia.

CULTURAL CONNECTIONS

The Philippines celebrates four months of Christmas: September, October, November, and December. This festive time includes many parades, concerts, parties, and decorations.

Elsewhere in Southeast Asia, such as in Malaysia and Indonesia, many people practice Islam, a **monotheistic** religion that was first spread by the prophet Muhammad. Muhammad collected messages he received from Allah, the god of Islam, into the Qur'an, the religion's holy book.

People in the Philippines are mainly Roman Catholic, a branch of the monotheistic religion Christianity that follows the teachings of Jesus Christ, who they believe was the son of God.

In China, Taiwan, South Korea, and Vietnam, Buddhism is often practiced along with Confucianism or Taoism. Confucianism is a philosophy based on the Chinese philosopher Confucius. He strongly believed in the importance of a moral code based on ethical standards, a well-ordered society, and respect for one's elders, ancestors, and the past.

monotheistic: Having to do with belief in one god.

Lunar New Year

In China, the most important day of the year is Lunar New Year, also known as Chinese New Year. Though this holiday always falls between January 21 and February 20, its exact date changes each year because it is based on the cycles of the moon. People celebrate by spending time with family, and many travel long distances to visit their relatives. Each lunar year is represented by an animal from the Chinese or Eastern **zodiac**. It's widely believed that the animal sign of the year in which you're born will influence your personality. Many other east and Southeast Asian countries celebrate the Lunar New Year in their own way. Some countries, such as Cambodia, celebrate even though they have a different new year date.

A street in Hanoi, Vietnam, prepares for Tet, the Vietnamese word for the Lunar New Year.

CULTURAL CONNECTIONS

In 2019, an outbreak of the deadly COVID-19 virus was first reported in Wuhan, Hubei Province, China. As the virus spread, people in China—and the wider world—were challenged to live in lockdown conditions, cancelling mass gatherings for important cultural holidays such as the Lunar New Year.

zodiac: An imaginary band in the sky that tracks the movement of planets; divided into 12 signs, each with a special name and symbol.

Torii gates represent holy Shinto areas. This torii off the coast of Miyajima, Japan, is famous for appearing to float on water.

Taoism is another philosophy that originated in China. It teaches the importance of living in harmony with nature. Much like Taoism, the Japanese religion Shinto promotes the relationship between human and nature by

Rohingya in Myanmar

When different groups living in the same place believe in different religions, conflict can sometimes arise. This is especially true if one group is an ethnic minority. One such conflict has been ongoing in Myanmar. The conflict is mainly between the Rohingya, who are mainly Muslim, and other ethnic groups, who are mainly Buddhist. The Myanmar government doesn't recognize the Rohingya as legal citizens, and they have been **oppressed** since 1962. Since 2017, Myanmar security forces have been carrying out a campaign of **ethnic cleansing** against the Rohingya. Thousands have been killed and hundreds of thousands have fled to Bangladesh.

oppress: To unjustly use power over another; to treat people in a cruel or unfair way.

ethnic cleansing: The practice of removing or killing people who belong to an ethnic group that is different from the ruling group in a country or region

Traditional offerings of flowers and food can be found around Ubud, Bali, where many people practice Balinese Hinduism.

worshiping the kami, which are spirits that can be found throughout life and nature. Many Japanese families celebrate seasonal changes and life events by worshiping at small Shinto shrines in their homes.

CULTURAL CONNECTIONS

For the Toraja people of Indonesia, death has a special set of traditions. Families care for the bodies of deceased loved ones until they can bring together distant family members for a proper funeral. This can take days, weeks, months, or even years.

On the islands of Bali and western Lombok in Indonesia, some practice Balinese Hinduism, another belief system that respects the natural world and the spirits of ancestors. Bali is home to thousands of temples meant for celebrating the religion's many holidays.

3 ART AND ARCHITECTURE

Many of the traditional art styles of east and Southeast Asia are heavily influenced by both cultural values and philosophical ideals. In east Asia, for example, Taoism and Shintoism both emphasize living in harmony with the natural world. These beliefs are often translated into art. One of the most recognizable styles in east Asia is the landscape, or painting showing nature from a wide angle.

In China, artists began to combine landscape paintings with **calligraphy**, which helped convey the artists' feelings about the landscape. In Japan, the most popular form of landscape art is the woodblock print, in which an image is carved out of wood and printed onto paper, often with the use of bright colors. **Bonsai** is also popular in this region as a reflection of the human connection to the natural world.

calligraphy: The art of making beautiful handwriting.
bonsai: The art of growing miniature trees in pots.

This woodblock print, created by Katsushika Hokusai in the 1830s, is one of the most well-known Japanese landscape pieces in the world.

Bonsai trees are grown by both professional and casual artists and gardeners all across Japan.

CULTURAL CONNECTIONS

Some bonsai trees outlive the artists that cultivate them. The oldest known bonsai tree in the world is about 1,000 years old.

In much of east and Southeast Asia, artists have built Buddhist temples that have stood for thousands of years. Buddhist temples come in many different varieties, and while these structures are found throughout Asia,

Anime: Past Meets Future

Born in Japan but now popular worldwide, anime sets itself apart from other forms of animation. The anime aesthetic, or style, includes vivid colors, ornate outfits, exaggerated features and expressions, and gravity-defying hair. These characteristics are rooted in Japan's traditional art forms of Kabuki theater and woodblock prints. Even more important to defining anime is the content. Audiences love the challenges that anime presents, as the stories are often unpredictable and complex. Anime is able to tackle the problems facing society and let authors express their creativity in a way that live action simply cannot.

Popular anime characters such as Totoro have helped spread Japan's unique animation style to the world.

the characteristics of each country's temples differ. While temples are often active places of worship, they also communicate values through their architecture. Each Buddhist temple is designed to symbolize the four elements: fire, air, earth, and water. A temple's square base represents the earth, and its highest point represents wisdom. Most Buddhist temples also contain images or statues of Buddha.

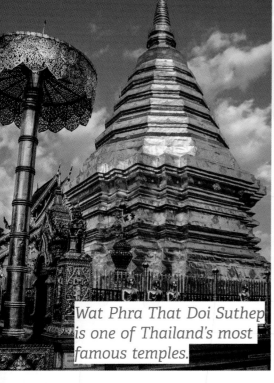

Wat Phra That Doi Suthep is one of Thailand's most famous temples.

Hong Kong's Nan Lian Garden features the famous Pavilion of Absolute Perfection.

K-Pop: A Global Sensation

Since the late 1990s, the musical genre known as K-pop—Korean pop—has been growing in popularity around the world. Defined mostly by its powerful supergroups, catchy beats, and a repetitive chorus, all accompanied by a synchronized dance, K-pop is much more than just a passing fad. K-pop stars are discovered by talent agencies and groomed from an early age to become superstars. Many practice for hours every day perfecting their singing skills and dance moves. Some even learn foreign languages to appeal to worldwide audiences. In 2019, the most popular K-pop boy band, BTS, sold around 300,000 tickets to stadium shows in the United States alone.

The K-pop supergroup BTS has risen in popularity along with the entire genre.

Along with the visual arts of painting, printmaking, and architecture, the dramatic arts hold an important place in east and Southeast Asia. Asia has a long history of theatrical dance, which varies by country but is always accompanied by traditional music and costume. Many countries' theatrical dances emphasize small gestures of the head, eyes, and hands, and they often tell stories, act out prayers, or recount myths.

CULTURAL CONNECTIONS

The Giant Buddha of Leshan in China is the largest Buddha sculpture in the world, standing 233 feet (71 m) tall.

Indonesia's most influential and well-known art takes the form of two traditional dances: the ordered dancing that is native to the island of Java and colorful, dramatic Balinese folk dances. In Malaysia, *mak yong* is a traditional drama in which Malay performers present heroic stories of sultans and princesses, accompanied by an orchestra that includes gongs and drums.

4 POLITICS AND HUMAN RIGHTS

T he types of governments in east and Southeast Asian countries are as varied as their cultures. In Japan, the government is similar to the government of the United Kingdom. Japan is a constitutional monarchy, a type of **limited government** that recognizes the emperor as a symbol of the nation. However, much of the power is given to the people, who can vote for officials once they reach the age of 18. Japanese citizens are granted freedom of speech, freedom of religion, and freedom of the press.

Thailand, Cambodia, and Malaysia also operate as constitutional monarchies. In both

limited government: A type of government led by the citizens of a country in which everyone, including all authority figures, must obey the law.

Cambodia and Malaysia, as in Japan, the monarch's role is mostly ceremonial. In Thailand, the king holds limited political power, along with a prime minister and a national assembly. However, each nation's elected government holds most of the political power. Most countries in east and Southeast Asia hold elections, but many countries—including Cambodia, Laos, Vietnam, and North Korea—have a **one-party system**. This means that citizens can vote for elected officials, but a single political party decides on the candidates citizens can vote for.

Prime Minister Shinzo Abe holds Japan's highest elected office as of 2020.

Many mourners in Thailand paid their respects to King Bhumibol Adulyadej after his death.

In South Korea, citizens also vote for representatives and are entitled to certain freedoms, though the South Korean government maintains the ability to limit its people's rights in cases of national emergency.

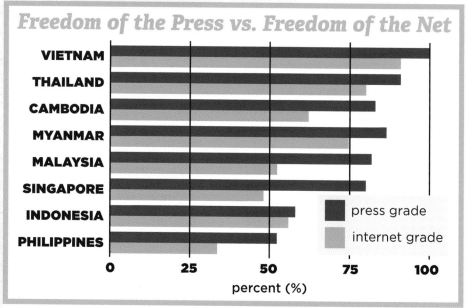

This graph, based on a Freedom on the Net 2017 report, shows the "grades" U.S.-based human rights organization Freedom House gives to different countries for freedom of press and internet in the countries of Southeast Asia.

The Khmer Rouge Regime

From 1975 to 1979, Cambodia was ruled by the Khmer Rouge, a brutal group rooted in **communism**. The party had been active since the 1950s, and in the 1960s, its leader, Pol Pot, organized the group to fight the Cambodian government. The Khmer Rouge wanted to turn Cambodia into an **agrarian** state that wouldn't have social classes. Pol Pot got rid of currency, trade, banks, and private property. The Khmer Rouge forced millions of people living in the cities to relocate to rural labor camps and enforced their laws and regulations through terror and **genocide.** Between 1 and 3 million people, or more than 25 percent of the population of Cambodia, died during the party's time in power. Today, many of the people who led the genocide still hold government positions.

Pol Pot's Khmer Rouge government was responsible for millions of deaths in Cambodia.

communism: A way of organizing society where there is no privately owned

Though communism is part of the governments of Vietnam, China, and North Korea, each government runs very differently.

Mao Zedong (1893–1976) was a communist revolutionary and founding father of the People's Republic of China.

Vietnam's constitution officially establishes it as a socialist nation, and political power is based on **democratic centralism**. In this system, the highest power comes from the top of the Communist Party of Vietnam and flows downward through a tight political structure. Though elected officials rule China, citizens' freedom of speech is very limited and a lot of internet content is censored. Citizens of North Korea have even fewer (**human rights**) than those in China. North

Sukarno and Pancasila

The first president of Indonesia, who served from 1945 to 1967, was named Sukarno. In 1927, he founded the Indonesian National Party, which helped end Dutch colonial rule. As president, Sukarno worked hard to unify the many islands of Indonesia. This is how he developed the set of five beliefs called Pancasila: belief in one god, humanitarianism, the unity of Indonesia, democracy based on debate and agreement among representatives, and social justice. Sukarno made Pancasila an official state philosophy. Although some Islamic organizations object to Pancasila being more important than their religious beliefs in the eyes of the government, Indonesian law requires all organizations to adopt these five principles.

human rights: Universal rights possessed by all people in the world because

Korea is a **dictatorship** led by Kim Jong-un. Its constitution guarantees freedom of the press, religion, and speech, but North Korea has an **unlimited government** and the people have very few rights and freedoms.

Soldiers bow to a statue of Kim Il-sung, the first dictator of North Korea.

dictatorship: A government in which the leader rules the country by force.
unlimited government: A type of government in which control is placed solely with the ruler and their appointees, and there are no limits imposed on their authority.

5

THE URBAN, RURAL, AND NATURAL ENVIRONMENT

Because east and Southeast Asia covers such a broad area, the climate and the natural landscape varies across these regions' many countries. Climate can also vary greatly within a country itself. For instance, in the **archipelago** of Japan, the islands to the south experience hot summers and mild winters, while the islands in the north experience freezing winters and cool summers. North and South Korea experience warm-to-hot summers, cool-to-cold winters, and a lot of rain. The whole country, however, gets a lot of seasonal rain because of a powerful **monsoon** system.

monsoon: Seasonal winds that affect climate in the southern areas of Asia, resulting in wet spring and summer months and dry winter months.

These major cities in east and Southeast Asia are urban hubs of culture with booming populations.

Mount Fuji is Japan's tallest peak. It's also an active volcano.

As one of the region's most developed cities, Seoul, South Korea, has many features seen in big cities worldwide.

Countries like Japan and South Korea are often considered **more developed**. In these countries, people mainly live in in modern apartment buildings in cities or suburbs. Japan isn't without its natural challenges, however. Japan is located in the **Ring of Fire**. Its landscape includes many mountains and volcanoes because of the **tectonic plates** moving beneath its islands. The nation experiences 1,500 earthquakes a year, and it contains more than 100 active volcanoes. People have to build with natural disasters, like earthquakes, in mind.

CULTURAL CONNECTIONS

Japan, Indonesia, and the Philippines all lie along the Ring of Fire. Though it makes up only 1 percent of Earth's surface, the Ring of Fire has more than half of the world's active volcanoes.

more developed: Having more modern features than other areas.

Ring of Fire: An area where large numbers of earthquakes and volcanic eruptions occur in the basin of the Pacific Ocean.

Monsoon Seasons

The climates of east and Southeast Asian countries are determined by the Asian monsoon, the largest monsoon system in the world. A monsoon from the north in the winter causes cold, dry weather in east Asia. In the summer, the monsoon switches direction and brings warmer air from the south and southeast, making the season very hot and humid. In Southeast Asia, monsoons cause not only the high temperatures that last from April to October but also bring the rainy season, which runs from May to October. Though the rainy season brings a lot of flooding to nations in this region, destroying structures and interrupting everyday life, Southeast Asians rely on the rainy season for water.

Monsoon flooding like this is common throughout Southeast Asia during the rainy season.

China is one of the largest countries in the world, and its climate and natural landscape vary. The country has a subarctic climate in the north, tropical climate in the south, and the Gobi Desert in the west. As in South Korea and Japan, Chinese urban centers are highly populated, and many citizens live in apartment buildings. In the countryside, houses are generally made of either clay bricks or stone.

CULTURAL CONNECTIONS

As of 2018, Tokyo, Japan, was the world's most populated city, with more than 37 million residents. It is expected to drop to number two by 2030, with its spot taken by Delhi, India.

The climate of Southeast Asia is mainly tropical, with most of the year being very hot and part of the year being very rainy. Many families in the **newly developed** countries of Indonesia, Malaysia, Thailand, Vietnam, and the Philippines live in urban areas. However, there are also many rural villages in these countries

newly developed: Having an increasing number of modern features.

The 2011 Tsunami

On March 11, 2011, a magnitude-9.1 earthquake occurred about 231 miles (371.8 km) northeast of Tokyo in the Pacific Ocean. It was the largest earthquake ever to hit Japan and caused a **tsunami** with 30-foot (9.1-m) waves to come crashing down on the Pacific coast of Japan's largest island, Honshu. More than 22,000 people were confirmed dead or declared missing after the disaster. In addition to the human cost, the event destroyed many homes, businesses, and farms. It also caused a nuclear emergency by damaging nearby nuclear power plants that then released dangerous amounts of radioactivity. It was one of the worst disasters in Japanese history.

The 2011 Japanese earthquake and tsunami caused widespread death and destruction.

tsunami: A series of large ocean waves, caused by an earthquake along the floor of the ocean.

as well as in the **less developed** nations of Cambodia, Laos, Timor-Leste, and Myanmar. Rural farming or fishing communities in Southeast Asia often live in wooden or bamboo huts on stilts with thatched palm roofs. The stilts prevent flooding in the rainy season and increase airflow during the hotter parts of the year.

This Cambodian village's houses are built on stilts to avoid flooding.

less developed: Not as built up or modern as other places.

6
SPREADING CULTURE THROUGH CUISINE

I t's impossible to talk about food in east and Southeast Asia without mentioning rice. Rice is not only the staple crop of Asia, it's also a huge part of how society and traditions have developed. Throughout history, this food has shaped social structures and traditional religions. In some places in Southeast Asia, sacred rituals involving rice have been created. Many Indonesian societies still make offerings to the Rice Mother, or goddess of rice. In Japan, the word *gohan* means both "cooked rice" and "meal."

CULTURAL CONNECTIONS

The Chinese have been using chopsticks since around 1200 BC.

In some places, rice is grown in terraced fields similar to this one in Vietnam. Terraces are horizontal ridges cut into hillsides for farming.

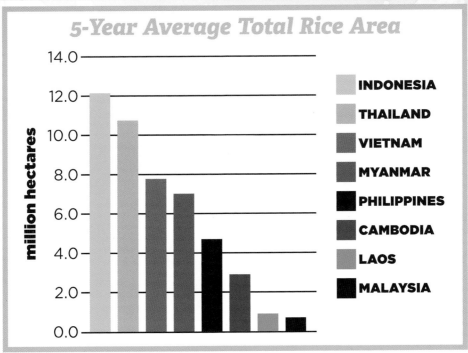

5-Year Average Total Rice Area

million hectares

14.0
12.0
10.0
8.0
6.0
4.0
2.0
0.0

INDONESIA
THAILAND
VIETNAM
MYANMAR
PHILIPPINES
CAMBODIA
LAOS
MALAYSIA

This graph adapted from U.S. Department of Agriculture data shows just how much land in Southeast Asia is used for rice production.

Street Food Capital of the World

Though Southeast Asia does have traditional sit-down restaurants, there's also been a recent rise in street carts selling regional favorites to locals and tourists alike. "Street food" typically describes traditional dishes made with local ingredients and often sold for a low price. Street food stalls are generally owned by families and give locals who don't have much time to cook access to quick, cheap, homemade food. Street food also gives visitors a great way to sample local cuisine and support small business in the country they're visiting.

Street food markets such as this are common sights across east and Southeast Asia.

As in many world cultures, meals have traditionally been an important source of family time in east and Southeast Asia. Most homes in these regions serve meals family style, with every person at the table encouraged to take a serving from a larger shared dish. Although grocery stores are becoming more widespread, many rural families continue to buy fresh ingredients at local markets.

This spread of Korean food is served family style, as are most meals in the region.

CULTURAL CONNECTIONS

Rice can take many forms, including rice noodles, rice crackers, and rice cakes—all of which are popular across east and Southeast Asia and beyond.

East Asian cooking can vary widely. Japanese cuisine features both fried foods, such as tempura, and raw foods, such as sushi. Korean foods are often grilled and based around pickled foods such as **kimchi**. In Southeast Asia, curries made with coconut milk are very popular, as is the use of herbs such as cilantro, mint, and holy basil. East and Southeast Asian dishes can be very spicy, and many regional dishes use hot chilies that grow well in the local climate.

Southeast Asian cuisine often reflects the nations that colonized the region. For example, Spanish-style **paellas** and **empanadas** are popular in the Philippines. The traditional Vietnamese sandwich banh mi is served on a baguette, sometimes with pâté. These two ingredients were introduced by the French.

kimchi: A spicy Korean vegetable dish that consists of one or more pickled and fermented vegetables and various seasonings.

paella: A Spanish dish of rice, meat, seafood, vegetables, and spices.

Worldwide Fast Food

You can probably recognize most of the fast food chains in east and Southeast Asia, but it might surprise you to know that you may not recognize what's on the menu. McDonald's in Thailand offers items such as chicken kaprao, or fried chicken in a sweet chili sauce. At Pizza Hut in Vietnam, you can order a pizza with seafood as a topping. At KFC in Malaysia, customers can find fried chicken with Thai spices. If you wanted breakfast at Burger King in China, you could order three kinds of congee, or rice porridge: chicken and soybean, mushroom and beef, or egg.

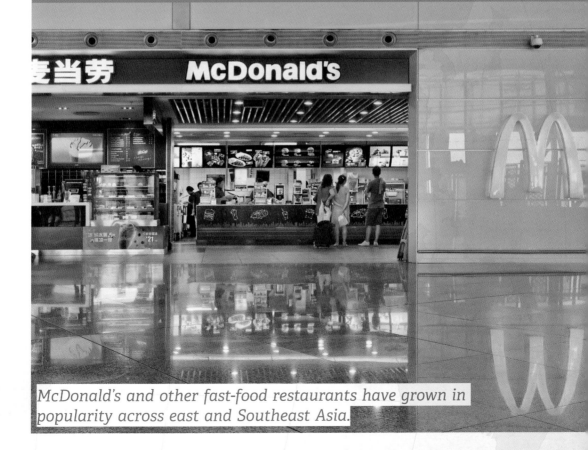

McDonald's and other fast-food restaurants have grown in popularity across east and Southeast Asia.

As globalization has increased restaurant options, younger generations of east and Southeast Asians have started eating out more and cooking less. Across Asia, fast food is becoming a popular option, with western chains such as McDonald's and Pizza Hut appearing across Asian cities.

This food vendor showcases colorful regional favorites.

East and Southeast Asia have experienced many different cultural influences through the centuries. From strong traditional roots to the significant effects of imperialism, these regions have produced totally unique cultures and practices. Food in east and Southeast Asia is just one effect of cultural diffusion. As the people of this region continue to blend their ancient history with modern development, there's no doubt their cultural contributions will continue well into the future.

GLOSSARY

agrarian: Of or relating to farms and farming.

archipelago: A group of islands.

Confucianism: The way of life as taught by Chinese philosopher Confucius.

democratic centralism: A communist party policy that allows members to discuss and debate as long as they follow decisions made at higher levels.

empanada: A turnover with a sweet or savory filling.

indigenous: Describing groups that are native to a particular region.

nirvana: The state of perfect happiness and peace, according to Buddhism.

one-party system: A type of government in which one political party has the right to form the government and other parties are either outlawed or only allowed limited participation in elections.

pilgrimage: A journey to a sacred place.

tectonic plate: One of the movable masses of rock that create Earth's surface.

FOR MORE INFORMATION

BOOKS:

Friedman, Mel. *Thailand*. New York, NY: Children's Press, 2015.

Mattern, Joanne. *East Asian Cultures in Perspective*. Hockessin, DE: Mitchell Lane Publishers, 2015.

Tyler, Madeline. *Cultural Contributions from East Asia: Fireworks, Tea, and More*. New York: PowerKids Press, 2019.

WEBSITES:

Ancient China
www.ancient.eu/china/
This fact-filled page contains a background on Chinese history and culture.

Countries of Asia
www.nationsonline.org/oneworld/asia.htm
Hosted by the Nations Online Project, this page has a directory for more information about Asian nations and regions.

Introduction to Southeast Asia
asiasociety.org/education/introduction-southeast-asia
This website features information about the lands, peoples, and cultures that can be found in Southeast Asia.

INDEX